Copyright © 2023 Samuel John

All rights reserved. No part of this publication may be reproduced, distributed, or transmitted in any form or by any means, including photocopying, recording, or other electronic or mechanical methods, without the prior written permission of the publisher, except in the case of brief quotations embodied in critical reviews and certain other noncommercial uses permitted by copyright law.

The word "volcano" comes from Vulcan, the Roman god of fire.

A volcano is an opening in the earth's crust through which magma is released.

👉 **What is magma?**

Is defined as molten rock found below the earth's surface.

Lava is magma that reaches the surface.

Volcanoes erupt due to increased pressure as magma heats up, spewing molten rock and gases into the air.

Its conical shape is due to the accumulation of magma expelled in previous eruptions.

In addition to magma, volcanoes also expel rocks, gases, and ash.

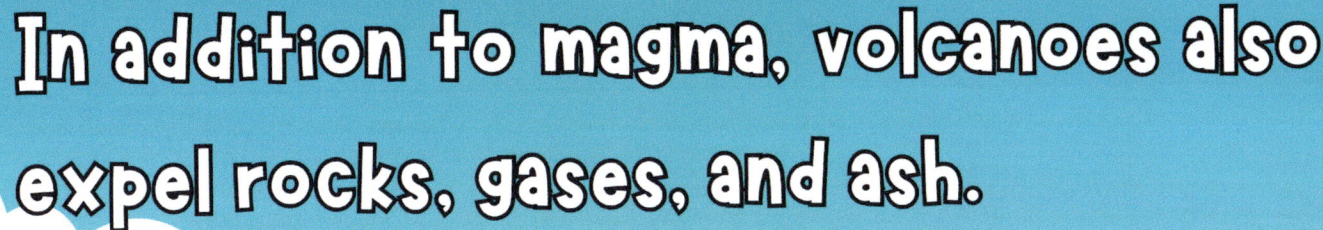

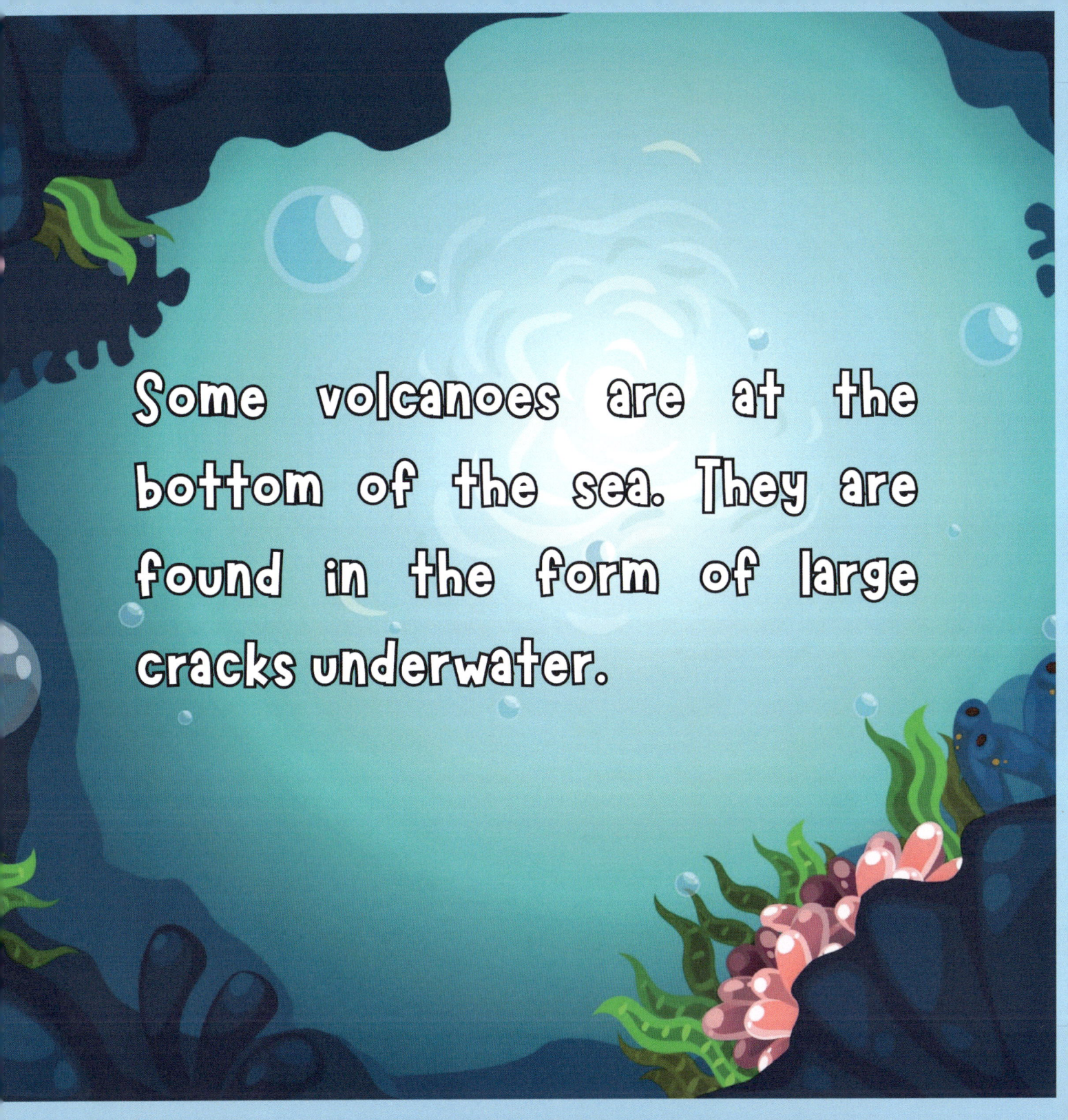

Some volcanoes are at the bottom of the sea. They are found in the form of large cracks underwater.

When volcanic eruptions happen at the bottom of the ocean, the accumulated lava may form volcanic islands.

Volcanoes can be very destructive. Ash and lava can destroy large tracts of forested areas, villages, etc.

There are 1,500 potentially active volcanoes on our planet.

The largest active volcano in the world is Hawaii's Mauna Loa.

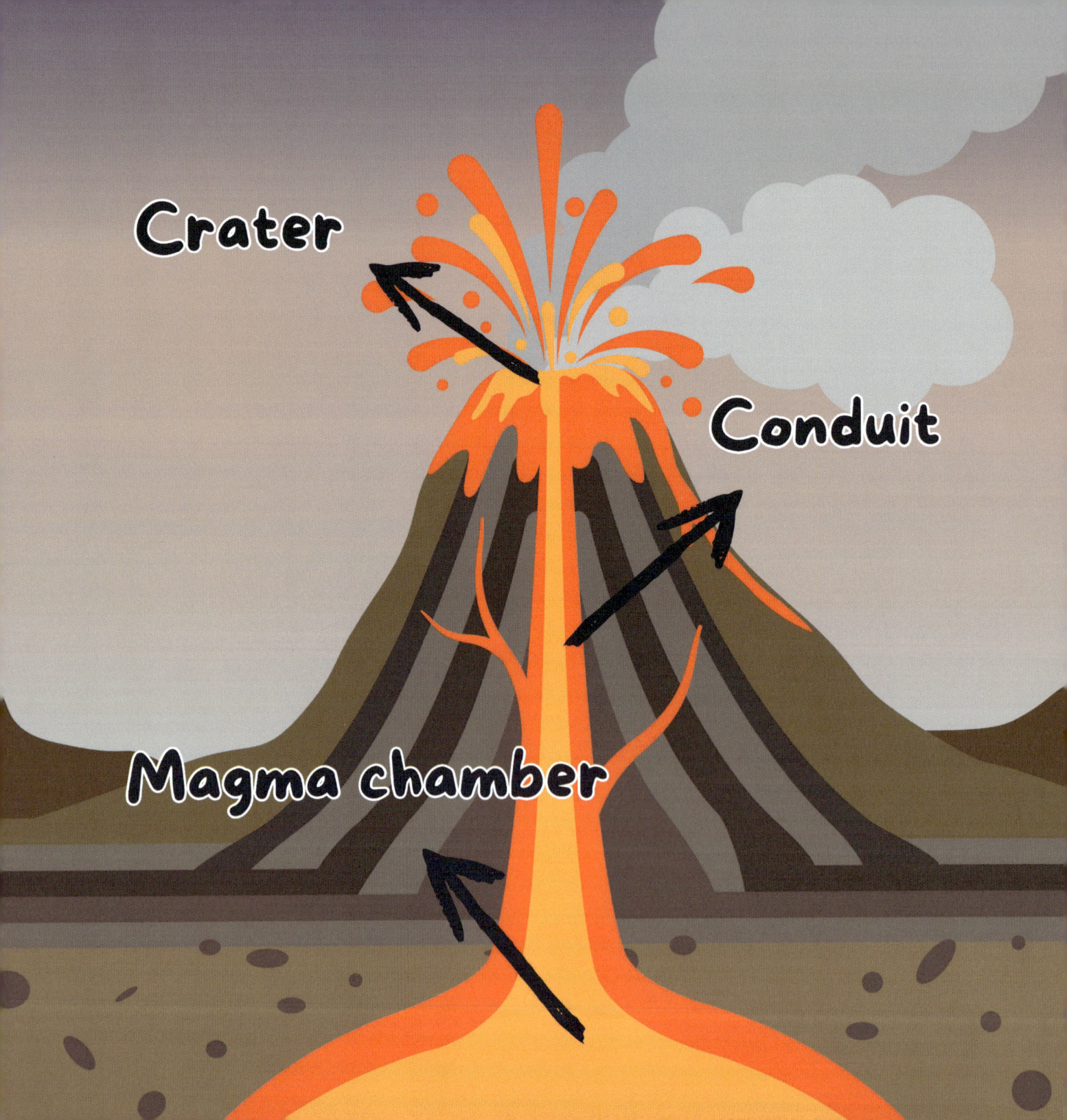

Parts of a Volcano

Magma chamber: This is the area beneath a volcano where magma collects before an eruption.

Crater: The hole through which lava, ash, and gases come out.

Conduit: Is the part that ejects lava and volcanic ash.

And here it ends!

I hope you liked it and learned new things.

Goodbye! Until next time!

I want to ask you a favor so that this book reaches more people, and that is that you rate it with a sincere opinion on the platform where you purchased it.

With that small gesture, you will be helping me to carry on with new projects.

I can't wait to start creating my next book for you!

You can leave your review directly here. It will only take you a few seconds.

www.bit.ly/volcanoes_review

Thank you in advance for taking time to share your experience. I appreciate your support!

See you soon!

KEEP LEARNING WITH OUR
EDUCATIONAL CHILDREN'S BOOKS

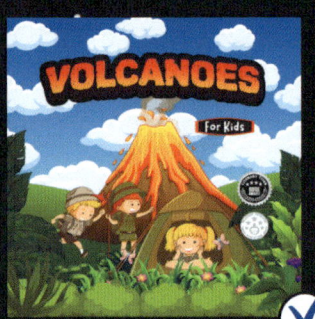
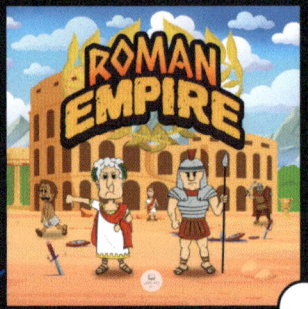

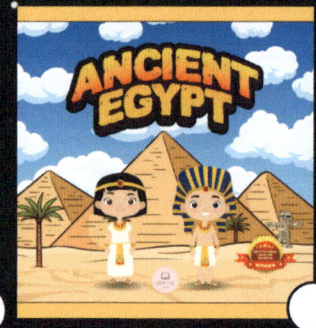

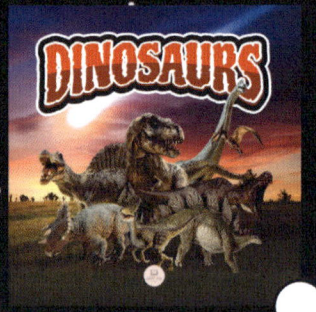
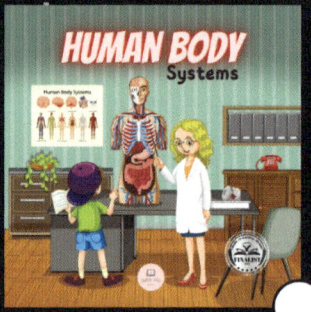
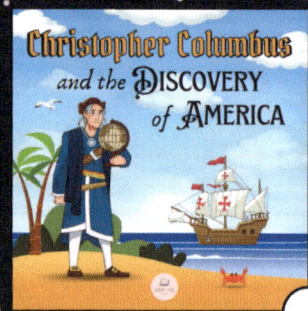

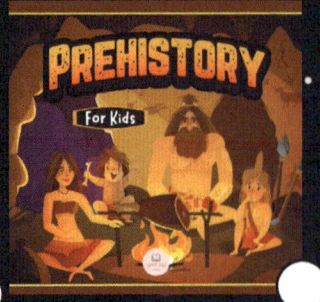
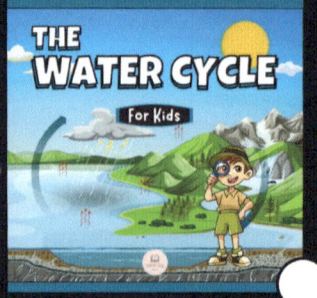

SCAN ME

https://www.pge.me/childrensbooks

Subscribe to my newsletter, receive 4 FREE BONUS, and stay informed of new publications, offers, and promotions of free books.

www.subscribepage.io/ebookfree

Bonus #1 - Free ebook "The The Steadfast Tin Soldier"
Bonus #2 - 19 Printable Halloween Coloring Pages
Bonus #3 - 50 Printable Mazes With Solutions
Bonus #4 - Free ebook With Sample Pages

This book comes to life with downloadable audio, perfect for engaging children and enriching their reading experience.

Printed in Great Britain
by Amazon